Ratio & Proportion

Allan D. Suter

McGraw Hill Contemporary

Series Editor: Mitch Rosin
Executive Editor: Linda Kwil
Production Manager: Genevieve Kelley
Marketing Manager: Sean Klunder
Cover Design: Steve Strauss, ¡Think! Design

Send all inquiries to:
McGraw-Hill/Contemporary
130 East Randolph Street, Suite 400
Chicago, Illinois 60601

ISBN: 0-07-287111-3

Printed in the United States of America.

1 2 3 4 5 6 7 8 9 10 QPD 09 08 07 06 05 04 03

The **McGraw·Hill** Companies

■ Contents

1. Simplify the ratio 9:15.

    Answer: _____

2. Write the ratio 24:36 in simplest form.

    Answer: _____

3. What is the ratio 56 to 8 in simplest form?

    Answer: _____

4. Write the ratio of 4 inches to 1 foot in simplest form.

    Answer: _____

5. What is the ratio of 9 feet to 1 yard in simplest form?

    Answer: _____

6. Express the ratio of 10 ounces to 1 pound in simplest form.

    Answer: _____

7. Write the ratio of 45 minutes to 1 hour in simplest form.

    Answer: _____

8. There are 12 men and 9 women in Maya's math class. What is the ratio of men to women in the class?

    Answer: _____

9. Lucas makes $31.50 in 3 hours. How much does he make in 1 hour?

    Answer: _____

10. Alexandra drove 120 miles on 5 gallons of gasoline. How many miles did she drive on one gallon of gasoline?

    Answer: _____

11. Solve for m in $\frac{5}{2} = \frac{m}{12}$.

Answer: _____

12. Write a proportion and solve for x if x is to 6 as 21 is to 14.

Answer: _____

13. Find the value of c in $\frac{c}{5} = \frac{14}{2.8}$.

Answer: _____

14. Write a proportion and solve for n if n is to 3 as 12 is to 5. Express the answer as a mixed number.

Answer: _____

15. Solve for y in $\frac{4}{5} = \frac{7}{y}$. Express the answer as a mixed number.

Answer: _____

16. A recipe calls for 3 tablespoons of butter for 12 cookies. How much butter is needed to make 36 cookies?

Answer: _____

17. The scale on a map shows that 1 inch = 80 miles. How far apart on the map are two towns that are 200 miles apart?

Answer: _____

18. Jerry got 2 hits for every 7 times at bat. Jerry was at bat 56 times. How many hits did he get?

Answer: _____

19. Max was paid $24.75 for working 3 hours. At this rate, how much did he earn in 6 hours?

Answer: _____

20. Six tickets cost $72. How much will 7 tickets cost?

Answer: _____

Evaluation Chart

On the following chart, circle the number of any problem you missed. The column after the problem number tells you the pages where those problems are taught. Based on your score, your teacher may ask you to study specific sections of this book. However, to thoroughly review your skills, begin with Unit 1 on page 7.

Skill Area	Pretest Problem Number	Skill Section	Review Page
Meaning of Ratio	1, 2, 3	7–16	17
Ratio Applications	4, 5, 6, 7	18–32	33
Ratio Problem Solving	8, 9, 10	34–41	42
Meaning of Proportion	11, 12, 13, 14, 15	43–55	56
Proportion Applications	All	57–63	64
Proportion Applications & Problem Solving	16, 17, 18, 19, 20	65–73	74

What Is Ratio?

Sometimes, you will need to compare one number with another number.

One way to compare numbers is to use a **ratio.**

Compare the number of circles to the number of triangles.

 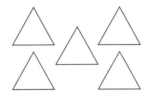

Ratios may be shown in three ways. All three ratios are read as "3 to 5."

$$3 \text{ to } 5 \qquad\qquad 3{:}5 \qquad\qquad \frac{3}{5}$$

The numbers in a ratio are called **terms.**

---

1. Compare the number of triangles to the number of circles.

   a) __5__ to __3__   b) ____ : ____   c) $\dfrac{\square}{\square}$

2. Compare the number of circles to the total number of figures.

   a) ____ to ____   b) ____ : ____   c) $\dfrac{\square}{\square}$

3. Compare the number of triangles to the total number of figures.

   a) ____ to ____   b) ____ : ____   c)

Write the Ratios

Write the three forms of ratios for each problem using the drawings above.

1. Number of circles to
   number of squares   a) __2__ to __3__   b) ____ : ____   c) ▢/▢

2. Number of squares to
   number of circles   a) ____ to ____   b) ____ : ____   c) ▢/▢

3. Number of circles to
   total number of figures   a) ____ to ____   b) ____ : ____   c) ▢/▢

4. Number of squares to
   total number of figures   a) ____ to ____   b) ____ : ____   c) ▢/▢

5. Total number of figures
   to circles   a) ____ to ____   b) ____ : ____   c) ▢/▢

Ratios as Fractions

It is easier to solve ratio problems when you write the ratios as fractions.

Write the ratio as a fraction.

1.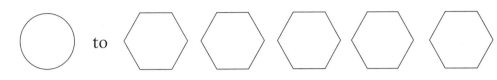

Compare circle to hexagons.

2.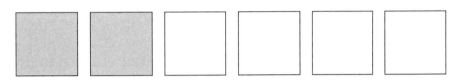

Show the ratio of shaded squares to total squares.

3.

Compare stars to rectangles.

4.

Compare the number of unshaded squares to shaded squares.

5.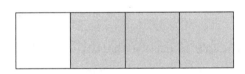

Compare squares to circles.

6.

Compare shaded shapes to all shapes.

Compare the Shapes

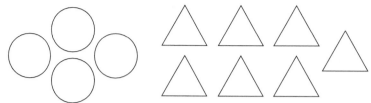

Use the drawings above to complete the problems.

1. ____ : ____ = $\dfrac{\square}{\square}$ Compare the number of circles to the number of triangles.

2. ____ : ____ = $\dfrac{\square}{\square}$ Compare the number of triangles to the number of circles.

3. ____ : ____ = $\dfrac{\square}{\square}$ Compare the number of circles to the total number of figures.

4. ____ : ____ = $\dfrac{\square}{\square}$ Compare the number of triangles to the total number of figures.

5. ____ : ____ = $\dfrac{\square}{\square}$ Compare the total number of figures to the circles.

6. ____ : ____ = $\dfrac{\square}{\square}$ Compare the total number of figures to the triangles.

Write a ratio for each of the following problems.

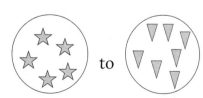

7. ____ : ____ = $\dfrac{\square}{\square}$

8. ____ : ____ = $\dfrac{\square}{\square}$

Draw the Ratios

1. Draw six Xs inside the rectangle. Circle one out of every three Xs.

   ← Write circled Xs to total Xs as a fraction.

2. Draw eight squares inside the rectangle. Shade three out of every four squares.

   ← Write shaded squares to total squares.

In comparing ratios, it is very important to keep the numbers in the same order as they are written.

Draw a picture for each ratio.

3. The ratio of stars to triangles is 3 to 5.

   stars   to   triangles

   stars
   triangles

4. The ratio of triangles to stars is 5 to 3.

   triangles   to   stars

   triangles
   stars

Write the Ratios as Fractions

Write a fraction to show how the first number compares with the second number.

1. $\dfrac{17}{30}$ There are 17 bicycles and 30 students.

2. $\dfrac{}{}$ There are 2 bicycles for every 3 students.

3. $\dfrac{}{}$ Fred paid $10 for 2 tickets.

4. $\dfrac{}{}$ Tauba drove 406 miles in 7 hours.

5. $\dfrac{}{}$ The wall had 5 feet of width for every 12 feet of height.

6. $\dfrac{}{}$ The store sells 120 tablets of aspirin for $8.00.

7. $\dfrac{}{}$ Jerry bought 3 ties for $36.

8. $\dfrac{}{}$ The box was 6 inches wide and 10 inches long.

Simplify the Ratios

When a ratio is written as a fraction, it is usually simplified.

$$4 \text{ to } 32 = \frac{4}{32} \div \boxed{\frac{4}{4}} = \frac{1}{8}$$

Write each ratio as a fraction and simplify.

1. $5 \text{ to } 20 = \frac{5}{20} = \frac{\square}{\square}$
   simplify

2. $12:15 = \frac{\square}{\square} = \frac{\square}{\square}$

3. $15 \text{ to } 30 = \frac{\square}{\square} = \frac{\square}{\square}$

4. $4 \text{ to } 12 = \frac{\square}{\square} = \frac{\square}{\square}$

5. $8:64 = \frac{\square}{\square} = \frac{\square}{\square}$

6. $6 \text{ to } 8 = \frac{\square}{\square} = \frac{\square}{\square}$

7. $8 \text{ to } 24 = \frac{\square}{\square} = \frac{\square}{\square}$

8. $16 \text{ to } 18 = \frac{\square}{\square} = \frac{\square}{\square}$

9. $9 \text{ to } 36 = \frac{9}{36} = \frac{\square}{\square}$
   simplify

10. $21:24 = \frac{\square}{\square} = \frac{\square}{\square}$

11. $7:49 = \frac{\square}{\square} = \frac{\square}{\square}$

12. $6 \text{ to } 18 = \frac{\square}{\square} = \frac{\square}{\square}$

13. $28 \text{ to } 35 = \frac{\square}{\square} = \frac{\square}{\square}$

14. $10 \text{ to } 25 = \frac{\square}{\square} = \frac{\square}{\square}$

15. $11:22 = \frac{\square}{\square} = \frac{\square}{\square}$

16. $5 \text{ to } 20 = \frac{\square}{\square} = \frac{\square}{\square}$

Denominator of 1

When a ratio is written as a fraction, it must have a denominator.

$$6:2 = \frac{6}{2} \div \frac{2}{2} = \frac{3}{1}$$ ← The denominator is 1.

Simplifying a ratio does not change its value.

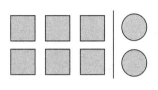

6:2

$$\frac{6}{2} = \frac{3}{1}$$

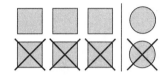

3:1

Write each ratio as a fraction and simplify.

1. 8:2 $= \frac{8}{2} = \frac{4}{1}$

2. 9:3 $= \dfrac{\square}{\square} = \dfrac{\square}{\square}$

3. 15:5 $= \dfrac{\square}{\square} = \dfrac{\square}{\square}$

4. 36:6 $= \dfrac{\square}{\square} = \dfrac{\square}{\square}$

5. 50 to 10 $= \dfrac{\square}{\square} = \dfrac{\square}{\square}$

6. 24:4 $= \dfrac{\square}{\square} = \dfrac{\square}{\square}$

7. 60 to 10 $= \dfrac{\square}{\square} = \dfrac{\square}{\square}$

8. 56 to 8 $= \dfrac{56}{8} = \dfrac{\square}{\square}$

9. 12:4 $= \dfrac{\square}{\square} = \dfrac{\square}{\square}$

10. 63 to 9 $= \dfrac{\square}{\square} = \dfrac{\square}{\square}$

11. 70:7 $= \dfrac{\square}{\square} = \dfrac{\square}{\square}$

12. 64:8 $= \dfrac{\square}{\square} = \dfrac{\square}{\square}$

13. 49 to 7 $= \dfrac{\square}{\square} = \dfrac{\square}{\square}$

14. 100:5 $= \dfrac{\square}{\square} = \dfrac{\square}{\square}$

Equal Ratios Are Equal Fractions

For every one X there are two circles. The ratio is 1 to 2.

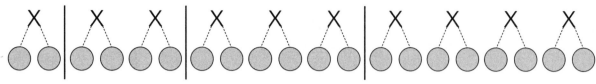

$$\frac{Xs}{circles} = \frac{1}{2} = \frac{2}{4} = \frac{3}{6} = \frac{4}{8}$$

$$\frac{1}{2} \times \begin{bmatrix} \frac{2}{2} \end{bmatrix} = \frac{2}{4} \qquad \frac{1}{2} \times \begin{bmatrix} \frac{3}{3} \end{bmatrix} = \frac{3}{6} \qquad \frac{1}{2} \times \begin{bmatrix} \frac{4}{4} \end{bmatrix} = \frac{4}{8}$$

Complete each set of fractions to make the ratios equal.

1. $\dfrac{1}{3} = \dfrac{2}{6} = \dfrac{3}{\square} = \dfrac{\square}{12} = \dfrac{5}{\square} = \dfrac{\square}{18} = \dfrac{7}{\square} = \dfrac{8}{\square} = \dfrac{\square}{27}$

$$\frac{1}{3} \times \begin{bmatrix} \frac{2}{2} \end{bmatrix} = \frac{2}{6}$$

2. $\dfrac{5}{1} = \dfrac{10}{2} = \dfrac{\square}{3} = \dfrac{20}{\square} = \dfrac{\square}{5} = \dfrac{30}{\square} = \dfrac{\square}{7} = \dfrac{\square}{8} = \dfrac{45}{\square}$

3. $\dfrac{3}{1} = \dfrac{6}{2} = \dfrac{\square}{3} = \dfrac{12}{\square} = \dfrac{\square}{5} = \dfrac{18}{\square} = \dfrac{21}{\square} = \dfrac{\square}{8} = \dfrac{27}{\square}$

$$\frac{3}{1} \times \begin{bmatrix} \frac{\square}{3} \end{bmatrix} = \frac{\square}{3}$$

4. $\dfrac{1}{5} = \dfrac{2}{\square} = \dfrac{\square}{15} = \dfrac{4}{\square} = \dfrac{\square}{25} = \dfrac{6}{\square} = \dfrac{\square}{35} = \dfrac{8}{\square} = \dfrac{9}{\square}$

Equivalent Ratios

Fill in the ☐ so that the ratios are equal.

1. $\dfrac{1}{2} = \dfrac{\boxed{}}{8}$

2. $\dfrac{5}{6} = \dfrac{15}{\boxed{}}$

3. $\dfrac{7}{8} = \dfrac{\boxed{}}{16}$

4. $\dfrac{1}{5} = \dfrac{\boxed{}}{45}$

5. $\dfrac{6}{7} = \dfrac{18}{\boxed{}}$

6. $\dfrac{3}{4} = \dfrac{\boxed{}}{20}$

7. $\dfrac{2}{9} = \dfrac{\boxed{}}{36}$

8. $\dfrac{4}{5} = \dfrac{\boxed{}}{25}$

9. $\dfrac{5}{\boxed{}} = \dfrac{1}{4}$

10. $\dfrac{18}{\boxed{}} = \dfrac{2}{5}$

11. $\dfrac{2}{\boxed{}} = \dfrac{1}{7}$

12. $\dfrac{\boxed{}}{49} = \dfrac{3}{7}$

13. $\dfrac{\boxed{}}{24} = \dfrac{3}{8}$

14. $\dfrac{5}{6} = \dfrac{\boxed{}}{12}$

15. $\dfrac{3}{4} = \dfrac{\boxed{}}{36}$

16. $\dfrac{5}{3} = \dfrac{10}{\boxed{}}$

17. $\dfrac{5}{4} = \dfrac{\boxed{}}{16}$

18. $\dfrac{\boxed{}}{64} = \dfrac{5}{8}$

19. $\dfrac{5}{7} = \dfrac{\boxed{}}{42}$

20. $\dfrac{3}{7} = \dfrac{21}{\boxed{}}$

21. $\dfrac{10}{\boxed{}} = \dfrac{2}{5}$

22. $\dfrac{1}{8} = \dfrac{5}{\boxed{}}$

23. $\dfrac{\boxed{}}{27} = \dfrac{1}{9}$

24. $\dfrac{3}{2} = \dfrac{\boxed{}}{4}$

Meaning of Ratio Review

Write the ratios as fractions.

1. There are 5 bottles of soda for 15 students.

2. The cafeteria sells 15 slices of pizza for $12.

3. The video store rents 3 videos for $10.

4. 3 sodas sell for $5.

5. The window is 3 feet wide and 6 feet tall.

Write each ratio as a fraction and simplify.

11. $4:8 =$

12. $6:36 =$

13. $5:50 =$

14. 3 to 30 =

15. 7 to 28 =

Simplify the ratios.

6. $21:28 =$

7. $4:16 =$

8. $10:15 =$

9. $11:44 =$

10. $8:40 =$

Complete the ratios so they are equal.

16. $\dfrac{3}{4} = \dfrac{\square}{20}$

17. $\dfrac{18}{\square} = \dfrac{3}{5}$

18. $\dfrac{3}{7} = \dfrac{18}{\square}$

19. $\dfrac{5}{3} = \dfrac{15}{\square}$

20. $\dfrac{5}{6} = \dfrac{\square}{24}$

Find a Pattern

A series of ratios form a pattern. Find the pattern and complete each table.

1. For every one can, there are three tennis balls.

Cans	1	2	3	4	5	6	7	8
Tennis Balls	3	6						

Think: $\dfrac{1}{3} \times \dfrac{2}{2} = \dfrac{2}{6}$

2. For every one pack of gum, there are five sticks.

Packs of Gum	1	3	5	7	9	11	13	15
Sticks of Gum	5				45			

Think: $\dfrac{1}{5} \times \dfrac{\square}{\square} = \dfrac{9}{45}$

3. For every one touchdown, a team gets six points.

Touchdowns	1	7	3	2	9	4	6	5
Points				12				30

Think: $\dfrac{1}{\square} \times \dfrac{2}{2} = \dfrac{2}{12}$

4. For every one dollar, you could get four quarters.

Dollars	1	3	7	2	10	6	9	4
Quarters		12	28					

Think: $\dfrac{1}{\square} \times \dfrac{\square}{\square} = \dfrac{3}{12}$

Fill in the Table

Complete the tables to show the amount paid for the number of hours worked.

1.

Hours Worked	1	2	3	8	40
Paid	$9		$27		

Think: $\dfrac{1}{9} \times \dfrac{\square}{\square} = \dfrac{3}{27}$

2.

Hours Worked	1	2	3	4	5
Paid	$8.75			$35	

Think: $\dfrac{1}{8.75} \times \dfrac{\square}{\square} = \dfrac{4}{35}$

3.

Hours Worked	1	8	10	40	80
Paid	$6.25				

4.

Hours Worked	1	4	8	20	40
Paid	$12.95				

From Words to Ratios

Ratios can be used to solve many problems. The first step is to write a statement as a ratio.

Sam worked 3 hours and earned $18.

Write a Ratio

$\dfrac{3}{18}$ ← hours ← dollars

Simplify

$\dfrac{3}{18} \div \dfrac{3}{3} = \dfrac{1}{6}$

Write each ratio in simplest form.

1. 8 miles in 2 hours
$\dfrac{8}{2} = \dfrac{\Box}{\Box}$

2. 3 eggs are needed to make 12 cupcakes.
$\dfrac{\Box}{\Box} = \dfrac{\Box}{\Box}$

3. $24 for working 3 hours
$\dfrac{\Box}{\Box} = \dfrac{\Box}{\Box}$

4. 4 gallons of paint for $72
$\dfrac{\Box}{\Box} = \dfrac{\Box}{\Box}$

5. 100 miles on 5 gallons
$\dfrac{\Box}{\Box} = \dfrac{\Box}{\Box}$

6. The box is 6 inches wide and 10 inches long.
$\dfrac{\Box}{\Box} = \dfrac{\Box}{\Box}$

7. 5 tickets cost $35.
$\dfrac{\Box}{\Box} = \dfrac{\Box}{\Box}$

8. Sue bicycled 27 miles in 3 hours.
$\dfrac{\Box}{\Box} = \dfrac{\Box}{\Box}$

Unit Rates

A unit rate shows a ratio with a denominator of 1.

> *Per* means *each* or *one*.

60 miles per hour means 60 miles each hour: $\frac{60}{1}$

32 feet per second means 32 feet each second: $\frac{32}{1}$

$3.25 per square yard means $3.25 for one square yard: $\frac{\$3.25}{1}$

Write each ratio in fraction form. Circle the word that tells you there is a denominator of 1.

1. $\dfrac{\boxed{}}{\boxed{1}}$ 50 miles (per) hour

2. $\dfrac{\boxed{}}{\boxed{}}$ 3 tennis balls per can

3. $\dfrac{\boxed{}}{\boxed{}}$ 9 revolutions each minute

4. $\dfrac{\boxed{}}{\boxed{}}$ 75 tablets in one bottle

5. $\dfrac{\boxed{}}{\boxed{}}$ 25 miles per gallon

Write as a Ratio in Fraction Form

Write a fraction to show how the first number compares with the second. If there is a word that tells you the denominator is 1, circle the word.

1. $\frac{46}{1}$ 46 miles (per) hour

2. —— Sue saves $48 in 5 weeks.

3. —— 7 compared to 20

4. —— 11 hits in 9 games

5. —— 1 out of 5

6. —— $7 per student

7. —— 1 ounce equals 28 grams.

8. —— 8 pounds for $9.85

9. —— 32 feet per second

10. —— 9:11

11. —— $25 for each shirt

12. —— 55 miles per hour

13. —— 5 items for $16

14. —— 36 miles per gallon

15. —— $2 per pound

16. —— 129 points in 8 games

17. —— $9 per hour

18. —— $5 per dozen

19. —— 17 students per teacher

20. —— $25 for working 3 hours

Writing Unit Rates

To find the unit rate of a ratio, simplify the fraction. The denominator must be 1.

Find the unit rate for each problem.

1. 85 miles on 5 gallons

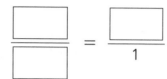

Unit rate: __17__ miles per gallon

5. 63 ounces in 9 cups

$$\frac{\boxed{}}{\boxed{}} = \frac{\boxed{}}{1}$$

Unit rate: _____ ounces per cup

2. 165 miles in 3 hours

$$\frac{165}{3} \div \frac{3}{3} = \frac{\boxed{}}{1}$$

Unit rate: _____ miles per hour

6. $21 for 3 tickets

$$\frac{\boxed{}}{\boxed{}} = \frac{\boxed{}}{1}$$

Unit rate: $_____ per ticket

3. 64 ounces in 4 cans

$$\frac{64}{4} = \frac{\boxed{}}{1}$$

Unit rate: _____ ounces per can

7. 360 miles in 8 hours

$$\frac{\boxed{}}{\boxed{}} = \frac{\boxed{}}{1}$$

Unit rate: _____ miles per hour

4. 56 apples in 7 boxes

$$\frac{\boxed{}}{\boxed{}} = \frac{\boxed{}}{1}$$

Unit rate: _____ apples per box

8. 120 miles on 5 gallons

$$\frac{\boxed{}}{\boxed{}} = \frac{\boxed{}}{1}$$

Unit rate: _____ miles per gallon

Comparing Unit Rates

Number Relation Symbols
< is less than
> is greater than
= is equal to

Write each statement as a ratio. Simplify each ratio to find the unit rate. Then compare the unit rates using the symbols above.

Fill in the symbol after you compare the unit rates.

1. 133 miles in 7 hours   108 miles in 6 hours

$$\frac{133}{7} = \frac{19}{1}$$ $$\frac{108}{6} = \frac{\square}{1}$$

Unit rate: ___19___ miles per hour ◯ **Unit rate:** _____ miles per hour

---

2. 72 miles on 3 gallons   120 miles on 5 gallons

$$\frac{72}{3} = \frac{\square}{1}$$ $$\frac{\square}{\square} = \frac{\square}{1}$$

Unit rate: _____ miles per gallon ◯ **Unit rate:** _____ miles per gallon

---

3. $60 for 4 tickets $90 for 5 tickets

$$\frac{\square}{\square} = \frac{\square}{1}$$ $$\frac{\square}{\square} = \frac{\square}{1}$$

Unit rate: $ _____ for one ticket ◯ **Unit rate:** $ _____ for one ticket

---

4. 425 meters in 5 hours   294 meters in 3 hours

$$\frac{\square}{\square} = \frac{\square}{1}$$ $$\frac{\square}{\square} = \frac{\square}{1}$$

Unit rate: _____ meters per hour ◯ **Unit rate:** _____ meters per hour

Find the Rates

Rates are ratios that compare different units of measurement.

Doug earns $6 per hour for mowing lawns. $6 per hour   6 : 1
How much will he earn in 4 hours?

You know that Doug earns $6 in 1 hour.   means
To find how much he earns in 4 hours, multiply. $6 × 4 = $24

Use your understanding of ratios to find the amounts below.

1. Jack earns $8 per hour.

   a) How much money would he earn in 3 hours? _____

   b) How much money would he earn in 8 hours? _____

2. If Tim drives 45 miles per hour,

   a) how many miles could he drive in 8 hours? _____

   b) how many miles could he drive in 4 hours? _____

3. Jan's car gets 23 miles per gallon.

   a) How many miles can she drive on 15 gallons? _____

   b) How many miles can she drive on 22 gallons? _____

4. Pork chops cost $1.39 per pound.

   a) How much will 3 pounds of pork chops cost? _____

   b) How much will 5 pounds of pork chops cost? _____

5. The material costs $8.25 per yard.

   a) How much will 3 yards of material cost? _____

   b) How much will 7 yards of material cost? _____

6. Taffy apples cost $5.00 per dozen.

   a) How much will 4 dozen cost? _____

   b) How much will 9 dozen cost? _____

Find the Cost

Apples $1.09 per pound

Film $1.45 per box

Cola $3.50 per 12-pack

Milk $1.42 per quart

Gasoline $1.73 per gallon

Candy $3.09 per bag

Use the rates from the pictures to complete the tables.

1.

Item	Cost
1 pound apples	a)
2 pounds apples	b)
3 pounds apples	c)
4 pounds apples	d)

3.

Item	Cost
1 gallon gasoline	a)
2 gallons gasoline	b)
11 gallons gasoline	c)
15 gallons gasoline	d)

5.

Item	Cost
1 sack candy	a)
2 sacks candy	b)
5 sacks candy	c)
7 sacks candy	d)

2.

Item	Cost
1 box film	a)
4 boxes film	b)
6 boxes film	c)
10 boxes film	d)

4.

Item	Cost
1 quart milk	a)
2 quarts milk	b)
4 quarts milk	c)
5 quarts milk	d)

6.

Item	Cost
1 12-pack cola	a)
3 12-packs cola	b)
4 12-packs cola	c)
6 12-packs cola	d)

Ratios as Rates

Use the information given to complete each problem.

3 items cost $12

1. a) How much will 6 items cost?
      $_____

   b) How much will 9 items cost?
      $_____

   c) How much will 12 items cost?
      $_____

3 tapes for $10

5. a) How much will 9 cost? $_____

   b) How much will 15 cost? $_____

   c) How much will 21 cost? $_____

$9 for 3 pairs of socks

2. a) 6 pairs will cost $_____.

   b) 9 pairs will cost $_____.

   c) 12 pairs will cost $_____.

2 candy bars for $1.35

6. a) How much will 6 cost? $_____

   b) How much will 10 cost? $_____

   c) How much will 16 cost? $_____

4 apples cost $.82

3. a) How much will 8 apples cost?
      $_____

   b) How much will 12 apples cost?
      $_____

   c) How much will 16 apples cost?
      $_____

5 cans of soup for $4.95

7. a) How much will 15 cans cost?
      $_____

   b) How much will 25 cans cost?
      $_____

   c) How much will 40 cans cost?
      $_____

$4.50 for 2 pens

4. a) How much will 4 cost? $_____

   b) How much will 6 cost? $_____

   c) How much will 8 cost? $_____

$4.25 for 3 ice cream cones

8. a) 9 will cost $_____.

   b) 15 will cost $_____.

   c) 27 will cost $_____.

Measurement Ratios

Sometimes you will need to compare measurements that are in different units (inches, feet, yards, etc.).

- First, write the measurements in the same units.

- Then, write a fraction ratio to compare the measurements.

<u>Compare</u>   <u>Simplified Ratio</u>

| 12 inches = 1 foot |
| 3 feet = 1 yard |

6 inches to 1 foot $= \dfrac{6 \text{ inches}}{12 \text{ inches}} = \dfrac{1}{2}$

Compare the following measurements as fraction ratios.

<u>Compare</u>   <u>Simplified Ratio</u>

1. 3 inches to 1 foot $= \dfrac{3 \text{ inches}}{12 \text{ inches}} = \dfrac{\Box}{\Box}$

    ↑ inches in 1 foot

2. 12 inches to 1 foot $= \dfrac{\Box \text{ inches}}{\Box \text{ inches}} = \dfrac{\Box}{\Box}$

3. 36 inches to 1 foot $= \dfrac{\Box \text{ inches}}{\Box \text{ inches}} = \dfrac{\Box}{\Box}$

4. 6 feet to 1 yard $= \dfrac{6 \text{ feet}}{3 \text{ feet}} = \dfrac{\Box}{\Box}$

    ↑ feet in 1 yard

5. 3 feet to 1 yard $= \dfrac{\Box \text{ feet}}{\Box \text{ feet}} = \dfrac{\Box}{\Box}$

6. 1 foot to 1 yard $= \dfrac{\Box \text{ foot}}{\Box \text{ feet}} = \dfrac{\Box}{\Box}$

Comparing Inches and Feet

Measurement ratios may be compared in the same units. To do so, change the larger units to smaller units.

	Compare	Simplified Ratio
12 inches = 1 foot	3 inches to 1 foot $= \dfrac{3 \text{ inches}}{12 \text{ inches}}$	$= \dfrac{1}{4}$

Change the feet to inches and write a ratio to compare.

Compare   Simplified Ratio

1. 4 inches to 2 feet $= \dfrac{4 \text{ inches}}{24 \text{ inches}} = \dfrac{\square}{\square}$

     ↑ inches in 2 feet

2. 3 inches to 1 foot $= \dfrac{\square \text{ inches}}{12 \text{ inches}} = \dfrac{\square}{\square}$

     ↑ inches in 1 foot

3. 10 inches to 5 feet $= \dfrac{\square \text{ inches}}{60 \text{ inches}} = \dfrac{\square}{\square}$

     ↑ inches in 5 feet

4. 12 inches to 3 feet $= \dfrac{\square \text{ inches}}{\square \text{ inches}} = \dfrac{\square}{\square}$

5. 9 inches to 1 foot $= \dfrac{\square \text{ inches}}{\square \text{ inches}} = \dfrac{\square}{\square}$

Comparing Feet and Yards

Measurement ratios may be compared in the same units. To do so, change the larger units to smaller units.

3 feet = 1 yard		

Compare   Simplified Ratio

2 feet to 1 yard $= \dfrac{2 \text{ feet}}{3 \text{ feet}} = \dfrac{2}{3}$

Change the yards to feet and write a ratio to compare.

Compare   Simplified Ratio

1. 4 feet to 4 yards $= \dfrac{\square \text{ feet}}{12 \text{ feet}} = \dfrac{\square}{\square}$

         ↑ feet in 4 yards

2. 3 feet to 2 yards $= \dfrac{\square \text{ feet}}{6 \text{ feet}} = \dfrac{\square}{\square}$

         ↑ feet in 2 yards

3. 6 feet to 5 yards $= \dfrac{\square \text{ feet}}{\square \text{ feet}} = \dfrac{\square}{\square}$

4. 5 feet to 10 yards $= \dfrac{\square \text{ feet}}{\square \text{ feet}} = \dfrac{\square}{\square}$

5. 2 feet to 6 yards $= \dfrac{\square \text{ feet}}{\square \text{ feet}} = \dfrac{\square}{\square}$

Comparing Ounces and Pounds

Measurement ratios may be compared in the same units. To do so, change the larger units to smaller units.

16 ounces = 1 pound	<u>Compare</u>	<u>Simplified Ratio</u>
	2 ounces to 1 pound = $\dfrac{2 \text{ ounces}}{16 \text{ ounces}}$	= $\dfrac{1}{8}$

Change the pounds to ounces and write a ratio to compare.

<u>Compare</u>   <u>Simplified Ratio</u>

1. 4 ounces to 1 pound $= \dfrac{\boxed{} \text{ ounces}}{16 \quad \text{ounces}}$ $= \dfrac{\boxed{}}{\boxed{}}$

  ↑ ounces in
  1 pound

2. 6 ounces to 3 pounds $= \dfrac{\boxed{} \text{ ounces}}{48 \quad \text{ounces}}$ $= \dfrac{\boxed{}}{\boxed{}}$

  ↑ ounces in
  3 pounds

3. 8 ounces to 2 pounds $= \dfrac{\boxed{} \text{ ounces}}{\boxed{} \text{ ounces}}$ $= \dfrac{\boxed{}}{\boxed{}}$

  ↑ ounces in
  2 pounds

4. 2 ounces to 2 pounds $= \dfrac{\boxed{} \text{ ounces}}{\boxed{} \text{ ounces}}$ $= \dfrac{\boxed{}}{\boxed{}}$

5. 10 ounces to 5 pounds $= \dfrac{\boxed{} \text{ ounces}}{\boxed{} \text{ ounces}}$ $= \dfrac{\boxed{}}{\boxed{}}$

Money and Time Ratios

Measurement ratios may be compared in the same units. To do so, change the larger units to smaller units.

<u>Compare</u>   <u>Simplified Ratio</u>

| 60 seconds = 1 minute | 5 seconds to 1 minute $= \dfrac{5 \text{ seconds}}{60 \text{ seconds}} = \dfrac{1}{12}$ |

Change the larger unit to the smaller unit and write a ratio to compare.

<u>Compare</u>   <u>Simplified Ratio</u>

1. 6 pennies to 2 dimes $= \dfrac{\boxed{}}{20}$ pennies pennies $= \dfrac{\boxed{}}{\boxed{}}$

    ↖ pennies in 2 dimes

2. 2 nickels to 1 dollar $= \dfrac{\boxed{}}{\boxed{}}$ nickels nickels $= \dfrac{\boxed{}}{\boxed{}}$

    ↖ nickels in 1 dollar

3. 2 quarters to 2 dollars $= \dfrac{\boxed{}}{\boxed{}}$ quarters quarters $= \dfrac{\boxed{}}{\boxed{}}$

4. 15 minutes to 1 hour $= \dfrac{\boxed{}}{60}$ minutes minutes $= \dfrac{\boxed{}}{\boxed{}}$

    ↖ minutes in 1 hour

5. 1 minute to 100 seconds $=$ seconds in 1 minute → $\dfrac{\boxed{}}{\boxed{}}$ seconds seconds $= \dfrac{\boxed{}}{\boxed{}}$

6. 50 seconds to 2 minutes $= \dfrac{\boxed{}}{\boxed{}}$ seconds seconds $= \dfrac{\boxed{}}{\boxed{}}$

Ratio Applications Review

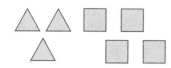

1. Compare the number of squares to triangles.

   a) __ to __   b) __ : __   c) □/□

Write each ratio as a fraction and simplify.

2. 13:26 = □/□ = □/□

3. 48 to 6 = □/□ = □/□

4. Make the ratios equal.

   $\frac{3}{8} = \frac{12}{□}$

Write each ratio in fraction form. Simplify when necessary.

5. A box is 8 inches wide and 12 inches long.

   □/□ = □/□

6. $45 for 3 shirts

   □/□ = □/□

7. Compare the unit rates.
   $25 for 5 tickets

   □/□ = □/1

   Unit rate: $_____ for one ticket

Use the information given to complete each problem.

| 3 tomatoes cost $1.29 |

8. a) How much will 5 tomatoes cost? $_____

   b) How much will 8 tomatoes cost? $_____

   c) How much will 10 tomatoes cost? $_____

Write a simplified ratio for each problem.

9. 15 inches to 2 feet = □/□ = □/□

10. 6 feet to 4 yards = □/□ = □/□

11. 12 ounces to 1 pound = □/□ = □/□

12. 10 nickels to 2 dollars = □/□ = □/□

13. 5 minutes to 1 hour = □/□ = □/□

$49 for 7 tickets

□/□ = □/1

Unit rate: $_____ for one ticket

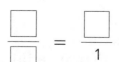

Ratio Applications

Start | 60 miles | Part 1 | 20 miles | Part 2 | 50 miles | Part 3 | Finish

Use the map above to answer questions 1 through 5.

Simplified

1. What is the ratio of
   Part 1 to the whole trip? _____ : _____

$$= \frac{\boxed{}}{\boxed{}} = \frac{\boxed{}}{\boxed{}}$$

2. What is the ratio of
   the whole trip to Part 2? _____ : _____

$$= \frac{\boxed{}}{\boxed{}} = \frac{\boxed{}}{\boxed{}}$$

3. What is the ratio of
   Part 3 to the whole trip? _____ : _____

$$= \frac{\boxed{}}{\boxed{}} = \frac{\boxed{}}{\boxed{}}$$

4. What is the ratio of
   the whole trip to Part 1? _____ : _____

$$= \frac{\boxed{}}{\boxed{}} = \frac{\boxed{}}{\boxed{}}$$

5. What is the ratio of
   Parts 1 and 3 to the whole trip? _____ : _____

$$= \frac{\boxed{}}{\boxed{}} = \frac{\boxed{}}{\boxed{}}$$

A recipe for punch calls for 3 pints of Hawaiian Punch, 4 pints of orange juice, and 5 pints of ginger ale.

6. What is the ratio of
   ginger ale to the whole drink? _____ : _____

$$= \frac{\boxed{}}{\boxed{}}$$

7. What is the ratio of
   orange juice to the whole drink? _____ : _____

$$= \frac{\boxed{}}{\boxed{}} = \frac{\boxed{}}{\boxed{}}$$

8. What is the ratio of
   the whole drink to orange juice? _____ : _____

$$= \frac{\boxed{}}{\boxed{}} = \frac{\boxed{}}{\boxed{}}$$

Using Ratios

4 pens for $6.00

How much do 8 pens cost?

Step 1: Write a ratio.   8:4

Step 2: Write as a fraction and simplify. $\frac{8}{4} = 2$ sets

Step 3: $6.00 × 2 = $12.00

How much do 6 pens cost?

Step 1: Write a ratio.   6:4

Step 2: Write as a fraction and simplify. $\frac{6}{4} = \frac{3}{2} (1\frac{1}{2})$ sets

Step 3: $\overset{3.00}{\cancel{\$6.00}} × \frac{3}{\underset{1}{\cancel{2}}} = $9.00

Use a ratio to solve the problems.

Special 2 for $4.98

1. a) How much will 4 pints of ice cream cost?

b) How much will 3 pints of ice cream cost?

Scarves 2 for $15.00

3. a) How much will 6 scarves cost?

b) How much will 5 scarves cost?

3 for $4.80

2. a) How much will 9 rolls of paper towels cost?

b) How much will 12 rolls of paper towels cost?

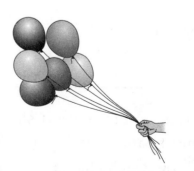

6 balloons for $10.00

4. a) How much will 24 balloons cost?

b) How much will 9 balloons cost?

Real-Life Ratios

2 pairs for $6.98

$19.95

3 pairs for $75.90

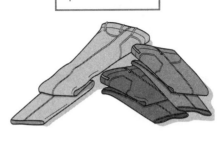

2 pairs for $28.88

Use the pictures to solve the problems.

1. How much will it cost for:

   a) One pair of pants? $_____

   b) One pair of socks? $_____

   c) One pair of shorts? $_____

4. How much will it cost for:

   a) 4 pairs of socks? $_____

   b) 3 pairs of shorts? $_____

   c) 4 pairs of pants? $_____

2. How much will it cost for:

   a) 6 pairs of shorts? $_____

   b) 3 sport shirts? $_____

   c) 8 pairs of socks? $_____

5. How much will it cost for:

   a) 3 sport shirts? $_____

   b) 3 pairs of socks? $_____

   c) 2 pairs of pants? $_____

3. If you want to buy 2 sport shirts, one pair of pants, and 2 pairs of shorts, how much change will you get back from $100.00?

   Answer: $_____

6. How much change will you get back from $20.00 if you buy one pair of shorts?

   Answer: $_____

Real-Life Practice

Use the pictures to solve the problems.

 2 pair for $36.66

 3 cans for $11.25

2 DVDs for $14.98

5 apples for $.95

---

1. How much will it cost for:

   a) One DVD? $_____

   b) One can of tennis balls? $_____

   c) One pair of shoes? $_____

   d) One apple? $_____

4. How much will it cost for:

   a) 5 DVDs? $_____

   b) 2 cans of tennis balls? $_____

   c) 4 pairs of shoes? $_____

   d) one dozen apples? $_____

---

2. How much will it cost for:

   a) 7 apples? $_____

   b) 4 DVDs? $_____

   c) 5 cans of tennis balls? $_____

   d) 3 pairs of shoes? $_____

5. How much will it cost for:

   a) 6 pairs of shoes? $_____

   b) 8 cans of tennis balls? $_____

   c) three dozen apples? $_____

   d) 9 DVDs? $_____

---

3. How much change will you get back from $20 if you buy 4 cans of tennis balls?

   Answer: $_____

6. How much change will you receive from $100 if you buy 5 DVDs, 2 pairs of shoes, and 6 cans of tennis balls?

   Answer: $_____

Seeing Ratios in Word Problems

Some word problems contain a ratio. These problems ask you to make a comparison.

Sam was at work for 9 hours. He took 2 hours for breaks. What was the ratio of his breaks to his hours at work?

Compare:

$$\frac{\text{break hours}}{\text{hours at work}} = \frac{2}{9}$$

   a) 2:7   **c)** 2:9

   b) 7:2   **d)** 9:2

Answer: **c)** 2:9

Circle the correct ratio for the problems below.

1. Scott repaired window sills for 5 hours. Out of 18 window sills, he repaired 15. What was the ratio between window sills fixed and hours worked?

   a) 5:15   **c)** 18:15

   b) 5:18   **d)** 15:5

3. In 7 days, Marty's Restaurant sold 74 dinner specials. The restaurant also sold 121 regular dinners. What was the ratio between dinner specials and regular dinners sold?

   a) 7:74   **c)** 121:7

   b) 121:74   **d)** 74:121

2. Janet's band played for 3 hours. They took two 30-minute breaks. What was the ratio between the length of the band's breaks and the hours played?

   a) 2:30   **c)** 30:3

   b) 3:30   **d)** 1:3

4. At basketball practice, Kathy shot 100 free throws. She made 82 shots, and missed 18. What was the ratio between the shots she missed and the shots she attempted?

   a) 82:100   **c)** 18:82

   b) 18:100   **d)** 100:18

Word Problem Practice

Solve these word problems that ask you to make a comparison.

1. Andrew makes $1,800 per month. He saves $300 and spends the rest. Write a ratio of the amount Andrew spends to the amount he saves.

_____ : _____

4. Write a ratio of the amount of consonants to vowels in the words NUMBER SENSE.

_____ : _____

2. It snows an average of 25 days in March at Ski-Town Ski Resort. Write a ratio of the number of days it doesn't snow to the number of days in the month.

_____ : _____

5. The Morristown Mongrels won 5 games out of the 13 they played. Write a ratio of wins to losses.

_____ : _____

3. A balloon vender is selling 9 red balloons, 4 blue balloons, and 8 yellow balloons. Write a ratio of red balloons to total balloons.

_____ : _____

6. In a class of 29 students, there are 15 boys. Write a ratio of the number of boys to girls.

_____ : _____

Ratio Relationships

1. What is the ratio of shaded squares to all squares? _____ : _____

2. What ratio represents the statement
   "seven out of nine square regions"? _____ : _____

3. If 6 pounds cost $5.40, what is the cost per pound? $_____

4. A pinch hitter was at bat 4 times and got 3 hits.
   Compare the number of hits to the number of times at bat. _____ : _____

5. The ratio of whales to dolphins is 9 to 3.
   How many whales are there per dolphin?

   _____ : _____ = _____ : _____ (simplified)

6. An item originally priced at $20.00 is reduced to $15.00.

   a) What is the ratio of the reduced price to the original price?

   _____ : _____ = _____ : _____ (simplified)

   b) What is the ratio of the amount saved to the original price?

   _____ : _____ = _____ : _____ (simplified)

7. If $\frac{1}{4}$ inch on a scale drawing represents
   5 miles, what does 1 inch represent? _____

8. Lana earns $7.95 per hour. How much does she earn in 8 hours? $_____

More Ratio Relationships

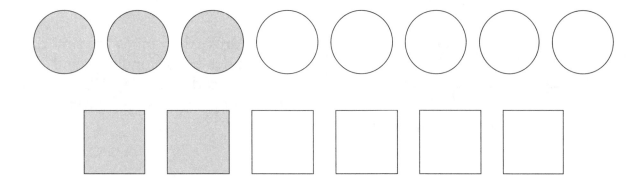

1. What is the ratio of shaded circles to all circles? _____ : _____

2. What is the ratio of circles to squares? _____ : _____

3. What is the ratio of shaded shapes to all shapes? _____ : _____

4. What is the ratio of shaded squares to all shapes? _____ : _____

5. What is the ratio of non-shaded circles to non-shaded squares? _____ : _____

6. A refrigerator was on sale for $450.00. The original price was $500.00. What is the ratio of the sale price to the original price?

   _____ : _____ = _____ : _____ (simplified)

7. If $\frac{3}{4}$ of an inch on a map is equal to 45 miles, what does 1 inch represent? _____

8. Justin earns $75 per week. How much does he earn in 30 weeks? $_____

Ratio Problem-Solving Review

Solve each problem. Simplify your answer.

1.

   What is the ratio of Xs to +s?

   _____ : _____

2. One inch on a map equals 150 miles. What do $3\frac{1}{2}$ inches represent?

   Answer: _____

3. Write the ratio of vowels to consonants in the word CONTEMPORARY.

   _____ : _____

4. During 7 days, Marie's Pizzaria sold 156 pizzas. They also sold 98 calzones. What is the ratio of pizzas to calzones?

   _____ : _____

5. Jesse drove 145 miles the first day, 330 miles the second day, and 275 miles the last day. What is the ratio of the first day to the whole trip?

   _____ : _____

6. If two pizzas cost $15.98, how much will 5 pizzas cost?

   Answer: _____

7. A car gets 45 miles to the gallon during highway driving and 34 miles to the gallon during city driving. What is the ratio of the car's city mileage to highway mileage?

   _____ : _____

8. Dorothy earns $2,450 per month. If she pays $725 each month in rent, what is the ratio of her rent to her income?

   _____ : _____

What Is a Proportion?

You can use a proportion to solve many different types of problems.

> A **proportion** is made up of two equal ratios.

You can multiply or divide to find equal ratios.

Multiply by a value of one.

$$\frac{2 \times}{3 \times} \boxed{\frac{2}{2}} = \frac{4}{6}$$

So, $\frac{2}{3} = \frac{4}{6}$ is a proportion.

Divide by a value of one.

$$\frac{6 \div}{9 \div} \boxed{\frac{3}{3}} = \frac{2}{3}$$

So, $\frac{6}{9} = \frac{2}{3}$ is a proportion.

Solve each proportion by finding the missing term.

1. $\dfrac{3 \times 2}{4 \times 2} = \dfrac{\boxed{}}{8}$

5. $\dfrac{4 \times 4}{7 \times 4} = \dfrac{\boxed{}}{28}$

9. $\dfrac{6 \div 3}{\boxed{} \div 3} = \dfrac{2}{9}$

2. $\dfrac{15 \div 5}{5 \div 5} = \dfrac{\boxed{}}{1}$

6. $\dfrac{\boxed{}}{6} = \dfrac{10}{12}$

10. $\dfrac{40}{100} = \dfrac{\boxed{}}{10}$

3. $\dfrac{1}{4} = \dfrac{3}{\boxed{}}$

7. $\dfrac{3}{\boxed{}} = \dfrac{15}{20}$

11. $\dfrac{9}{7} = \dfrac{18}{\boxed{}}$

4. $\dfrac{3}{2} = \dfrac{15}{\boxed{}}$

8. $\dfrac{\boxed{}}{10} = \dfrac{1}{2}$

12. $\dfrac{\boxed{}}{100} = \dfrac{3}{4}$

Simplify One Ratio

To find a missing term in a proportion, you may want to simplify one of the ratios.

EXAMPLE

Find the missing term.

$$\frac{3}{6} = \frac{\boxed{}}{8}$$

STEP 1

Simplify $\frac{3}{6}$ to $\frac{1}{2}$.

$$\frac{\overset{1}{\cancel{3}}}{\underset{2}{\cancel{6}}} = \frac{\boxed{}}{8}$$

STEP 2

Solve the missing term.

$$\frac{1}{2} \times \boxed{\frac{4}{4}} = \frac{\boxed{4}}{8}$$

> Think: What number do you multiply 2 by to get 8?

Simplify if necessary. Find each missing term.

1. $\dfrac{\overset{1}{\cancel{4}} \times 5}{\underset{2}{\cancel{8}} \times 5} = \dfrac{\boxed{}}{10}$

2. $\dfrac{6}{15} = \dfrac{8}{\boxed{}}$

3. $\dfrac{\boxed{}}{18} = \dfrac{5}{30}$

4. $\dfrac{8}{\boxed{}} = \dfrac{10}{15}$

5. $\dfrac{\boxed{}}{12} = \dfrac{\overset{3}{\cancel{6}}}{\underset{4}{\cancel{8}}}$

6. $\dfrac{\boxed{}}{24} = \dfrac{15}{20}$

7. $\dfrac{18}{\boxed{}} = \dfrac{30}{5}$

8. $\dfrac{15}{9} = \dfrac{\boxed{}}{12}$

9. $\dfrac{\overset{1}{\cancel{7}}}{\underset{3}{\cancel{21}}} = \dfrac{9}{\boxed{}}$

10. $\dfrac{10}{14} = \dfrac{\boxed{}}{21}$

11. $\dfrac{6}{2} = \dfrac{15}{\boxed{}}$

12. $\dfrac{30}{25} = \dfrac{\boxed{}}{15}$

Read the Proportion

A proportion is a statement that two ratios are equal.

Proportion

$$\frac{3}{4} = \frac{9}{12}$$

Read: "3 is to 4 as 9 is to 12."

Write the proportions as fraction ratios.

1. 2 is to 3 as 6 is to 9 $\qquad \dfrac{2}{3} = \dfrac{6}{9}$

2. 1 is to 4 as 2 is to 8 $\qquad \dfrac{1}{4} = \dfrac{\boxed{}}{\boxed{}}$

3. 7 is to 3 as 14 is to 6 $\qquad \dfrac{\boxed{}}{\boxed{}} = \dfrac{\boxed{}}{\boxed{}}$

4. 2 is to 5 as 4 is to 10 $\qquad \dfrac{\boxed{}}{\boxed{}} = \dfrac{\boxed{}}{\boxed{}}$

5. 5 is to 8 as 10 is to 16 $\qquad \dfrac{\boxed{}}{\boxed{}} = \dfrac{\boxed{}}{\boxed{}}$

6. 8 is to 12 as 4 is to 6 $\qquad \dfrac{\boxed{}}{\boxed{}} = \dfrac{\boxed{}}{\boxed{}}$

7. 50 is to 25 as 2 is to 1 $\qquad \dfrac{\boxed{}}{\boxed{}} = \dfrac{\boxed{}}{\boxed{}}$

Two Equal Ratios

Two ratios are equal when their **cross products** are equal.

| The cross products are: 2 × 6 and 4 × 3. | $\dfrac{2}{3} \times \dfrac{4}{6}$ | The cross products are: 1 × 9 and 3 × 3. | $\dfrac{1}{3} \times \dfrac{3}{9}$ |

$$2 \times 6 = 4 \times 3$$
$$12 = 12$$

$$1 \times 9 = 3 \times 3$$
$$9 = 9$$

Find the cross products for each problem.

1. $\dfrac{2}{3} \times \dfrac{6}{9}$

$$2 \times 9 = 6 \times 3$$

$$\underline{} = \underline{}$$

$$18$$

4. $\dfrac{8}{5} \times \dfrac{40}{25}$

$$\underline{} \times \underline{} = \underline{} \times \underline{}$$

$$\underline{} = \underline{}$$

7. $\dfrac{8}{3} \times \dfrac{16}{6}$

$$\underline{} \times \underline{} = \underline{} \times \underline{}$$

$$\underline{} = \underline{}$$

2. $\dfrac{7}{3} \times \dfrac{21}{9}$

$$\underline{} \times \underline{} = \underline{} \times \underline{}$$

$$\underline{} = \underline{}$$

5. $\dfrac{6}{18} \times \dfrac{12}{36}$

$$\underline{} \times \underline{} = \underline{} \times \underline{}$$

$$\underline{} = \underline{}$$

8. $\dfrac{7}{8} \times \dfrac{91}{104}$

$$\underline{} \times \underline{} = \underline{} \times \underline{}$$

$$\underline{} = \underline{}$$

3. $\dfrac{4}{5} \times \dfrac{16}{20}$

$$\underline{} \times \underline{} = \underline{} \times \underline{}$$

$$\underline{} = \underline{}$$

6. $\dfrac{5}{1} \times \dfrac{10}{2}$

$$\underline{} \times \underline{} = \underline{} \times \underline{}$$

$$\underline{} = \underline{}$$

9. $\dfrac{10}{15} \times \dfrac{30}{45}$

$$\underline{} \times \underline{} = \underline{} \times \underline{}$$

$$\underline{} = \underline{}$$

Cross Products

Two ratios are equal when their **cross products** are equal.

$$\frac{2}{3} \quad\times\quad \frac{4}{6}$$

$$2 \times 6 \qquad 4 \times 3$$

$$12 \quad = \quad 12$$

The cross products are equal:

So, $\frac{2}{3} = \frac{4}{6}$

$$\frac{2}{5} \quad\times\quad \frac{3}{4}$$

$$2 \times 4 \qquad 3 \times 5$$

$$8 \quad \neq \quad 15$$

The cross products are not equal:

So, $\frac{2}{5} \neq \frac{3}{4}$

- Use cross products to determine whether or not the ratios are equal.

- Use the symbols = (equal to) or ≠ (not equal to) in the ◯.

1. $\dfrac{1}{4} \quad\times\quad \dfrac{3}{12}$

$$1 \times 12 \qquad 3 \times 4$$

$$12 \quad \boxed{=} \quad \underline{}$$

4. $\dfrac{42}{56} \quad\times\quad \dfrac{7}{9}$

$$\underline{} \times \underline{} \qquad \underline{} \times \underline{}$$

$$\underline{} \quad \bigcirc \quad \underline{}$$

7. $\dfrac{5}{12} \quad\times\quad \dfrac{80}{192}$

$$\underline{} \times \underline{} \qquad \underline{} \times \underline{}$$

$$\underline{} \quad \bigcirc \quad \underline{}$$

2. $\dfrac{5}{6} \quad\times\quad \dfrac{2}{3}$

$$5 \times 3 \qquad 2 \times 6$$

$$\underline{} \quad \boxed{\neq} \quad \underline{}$$

5. $\dfrac{9}{13} \quad\times\quad \dfrac{63}{91}$

$$\underline{} \times \underline{} \qquad \underline{} \times \underline{}$$

$$\underline{} \quad \bigcirc \quad \underline{}$$

8. $\dfrac{4}{7} \quad\times\quad \dfrac{52}{91}$

$$\underline{} \times \underline{} \qquad \underline{} \times \underline{}$$

$$\underline{} \quad \bigcirc \quad \underline{}$$

3. $\dfrac{21}{28} \quad\times\quad \dfrac{3}{4}$

$$\underline{} \times \underline{} \qquad \underline{} \times \underline{}$$

$$\underline{} \quad \bigcirc \quad \underline{}$$

6. $\dfrac{7}{3} \quad\times\quad \dfrac{14}{6}$

$$\underline{} \times \underline{} \qquad \underline{} \times \underline{}$$

$$\underline{} \quad \bigcirc \quad \underline{}$$

9. $\dfrac{12}{15} \quad\times\quad \dfrac{24}{40}$

$$\underline{} \times \underline{} \qquad \underline{} \times \underline{}$$

$$\underline{} \quad \bigcirc \quad \underline{}$$

Proportion Readiness

If the cross products are equal, then the ratios are equal. Use cross products to see if the two ratios form a proportion.

Find the cross products. Write = (equal to) or ≠ (not equal to) in the .

1. $\frac{1}{2}$ = $\frac{5}{10}$

    $\boxed{10}$ $\boxed{10}$
    1×10 5×2

2. $\frac{3}{5}$ ≠ $\frac{2}{3}$

    $\boxed{9}$ $\boxed{10}$
    3×3 2×5

3. $\frac{4}{6}$ ◯ $\frac{12}{18}$

    ☐ ☐

4. $\frac{9}{8}$ ◯ $\frac{54}{18}$

    ☐ ☐

5. $\frac{6}{8}$ ◯ $\frac{9}{16}$

    ☐ ☐

6. $\frac{12}{3}$ ◯ $\frac{36}{9}$

    ☐ ☐

7. $\frac{8}{4}$ ◯ $\frac{32}{16}$

    ☐ ☐

8. $\frac{11}{13}$ ◯ $\frac{8}{12}$

    ☐ ☐

9. $\frac{8}{24}$ ◯ $\frac{3}{9}$

    ☐ ☐

10. $\frac{5}{8}$ ◯ $\frac{45}{72}$

    ☐ ☐

11. $\frac{18}{14}$ ◯ $\frac{9}{7}$

    ☐ ☐

12. $\frac{35}{4}$ ◯ $\frac{27}{3}$

    ☐ ☐

Find the Unknown Term

You can use cross products to find a missing number in a proportion. Use n to stand for the missing number.

> A missing number in a proportion is called a **term**.

To solve a proportion:
$$\frac{6}{27} = \frac{2}{n}$$

Step 1: Write the cross products. $\qquad\qquad\qquad\qquad 6 \times n = 2 \times 27$

Step 2: Multiply the two numbers in the cross product. $\quad 6 \times n = 54$

Step 3: Divide by the third number to find what n is. $\quad n = 54 \div 6$

Step 4: Solve for n. $\qquad\qquad\qquad\qquad\qquad\qquad n = 9$

Find the missing terms in the proportions below.

1. $\dfrac{3}{4} = \dfrac{n}{32}$

    $3 \times 32 = n \times 4$

    $96 = n \times 4$

    $96 \div 4 = n$

    $\underline{\hspace{2cm}} = n$

4. $\dfrac{n}{9} = \dfrac{2}{6}$

    $n \times 6 = 2 \times 9$

    $n \times 6 = 18$

    $n = 18 \div 6$

    $n = \underline{\hspace{2cm}}$

2. $\dfrac{8}{n} = \dfrac{2}{5}$

5. $\dfrac{n}{8} = \dfrac{15}{20}$

3. $\dfrac{n}{14} = \dfrac{3}{21}$

6. $\dfrac{n}{15} = \dfrac{4}{5}$

Solve and Check

In the proportion $\frac{6}{8} = \frac{n}{20}$, Sam got an answer of 15 for n and Jackie got an answer of 10 for n. Who was correct, Sam or Jackie?

	Sam's check	Jackie's check
Step 1: Write the solution for n.	$\frac{6}{8} = \frac{15}{20}$	$\frac{6}{8} = \frac{10}{20}$
Step 2: Cross multiply.	$6 \times 20 = 15 \times 8$	$6 \times 20 = 10 \times 8$
Step 3: Compare.	$120 = 120$	$120 \neq 80$
	⌐ correct	⌐ incorrect

Sam's answer is correct because the cross products are equal.

Solve for n. Check each answer by multiplying the cross products.

1. $\frac{4}{n} = \frac{3}{15}$

4. $\frac{n}{6} = \frac{6}{4}$

7. $\frac{15}{n} = \frac{2}{12}$

2. $\frac{9}{6} = \frac{15}{n}$

5. $\frac{12}{n} = \frac{15}{10}$

8. $\frac{12}{18} = \frac{2}{n}$

3. $\frac{28}{4} = \frac{n}{5}$

6. $\frac{10}{6} = \frac{n}{9}$

9. $\frac{14}{n} = \frac{21}{6}$

Apply Your Skills

Solve for n in the proportions below.

1. $\dfrac{1}{6} = \dfrac{n}{30}$

6. $\dfrac{n}{5} = \dfrac{18}{2}$

11. $\dfrac{3}{8} = \dfrac{n}{24}$

2. $\dfrac{9}{n} = \dfrac{6}{8}$

7. $\dfrac{4}{6} = \dfrac{10}{n}$

12. $\dfrac{8}{2} = \dfrac{12}{n}$

3. $\dfrac{n}{18} = \dfrac{5}{6}$

8. $\dfrac{100}{n} = \dfrac{5}{2}$

13. $\dfrac{n}{36} = \dfrac{8}{9}$

4. $\dfrac{25}{10} = \dfrac{15}{n}$

9. $\dfrac{5}{n} = \dfrac{1}{200}$

14. $\dfrac{2}{5} = \dfrac{n}{25}$

5. $\dfrac{7}{8} = \dfrac{n}{56}$

10. $\dfrac{4}{7} = \dfrac{16}{n}$

15. $\dfrac{2}{n} = \dfrac{3}{27}$

Proportions with Fractions

Find the missing term in the proportions below. Change all answers to mixed numbers.

1. $\frac{2}{3} = \frac{n}{5}$

   $2 \times 5 = n \times 3$

   $10 = n \times 3$

   $10 \div 3 = n$

   $3\frac{1}{3} = n$

5. $\frac{8}{7} = \frac{9}{n}$

   $8 \times n = 9 \times 7$

   $8 \times n = 63$

   $n = 63 \div 8$

   $n = \underline{\hspace{1cm}}$

2. $\frac{n}{3} = \frac{8}{5}$

6. $\frac{8}{7} = \frac{n}{8}$

3. $\frac{3}{7} = \frac{5}{n}$

7. $\frac{n}{6} = \frac{3}{5}$

4. $\frac{6}{n} = \frac{4}{7}$

8. $\frac{9}{n} = \frac{4}{7}$

Proportions with Decimals

Use the cross-product method to solve proportions with decimals in them.

1. $\dfrac{3}{4} = \dfrac{3.6}{n}$

     $3 \times n = 3.6 \times 4$

     $3 \times n = 14.4$

         $n = 14.4 \div 3$

         $n = 4.8$

5. $\dfrac{5}{2.5} = \dfrac{n}{17.5}$

   $5 \times 17.5 = n \times 2.5$

        $87.5 = n \times 2.5$

  $87.5 \div 2.5 = n$

     $\rule{2cm}{0.4pt} = n$

2. $\dfrac{n}{1.2} = \dfrac{6}{3.6}$

6. $\dfrac{.14}{.28} = \dfrac{3}{n}$

3. $\dfrac{7}{n} = \dfrac{5}{9.35}$

7. $\dfrac{8}{n} = \dfrac{13}{2.6}$

4. $\dfrac{n}{2} = \dfrac{3.54}{3}$

8. $\dfrac{6}{1.26} = \dfrac{n}{2.52}$

Missing Term

Write a proportion for each sentence and solve for the missing term.

<u>Sentence</u>	<u>Proportion</u>	<u>Missing Term</u>

1. 3 is to 4 as n is to 16 $\qquad$ $\dfrac{3}{4} = \dfrac{n}{16}$ $\qquad$ $n =$ _____

whole number

2. 4 is to 6 as 10 is to n $\qquad$ $\dfrac{\Box}{\Box} = \dfrac{\Box}{\Box}$ $\qquad$ _____

whole number

3. n is to 20 as 5 is to 8 $\qquad$ $\dfrac{\Box}{\Box} = \dfrac{\Box}{\Box}$ $\qquad$ _____

mixed number

4. 2.5 is to n as 15 is to 18 $\qquad$ $\dfrac{\Box}{\Box} = \dfrac{\Box}{\Box}$ $\qquad$ _____

whole number

5. 2.78 is to 2 as n is to 5 $\qquad$ $\dfrac{\Box}{\Box} = \dfrac{\Box}{\Box}$ $\qquad$ _____

decimal

6. 8 is to 5 as 13 is to n $\qquad$ $\dfrac{\Box}{\Box} = \dfrac{\Box}{\Box}$ $\qquad$ _____

mixed number

7. 3.25 is to 1 as n is to 6 $\qquad$ $\dfrac{\Box}{\Box} = \dfrac{\Box}{\Box}$ $\qquad$ _____

decimal

8. n is to 4 as 15 is to 6 $\qquad$ $\dfrac{\Box}{\Box} = \dfrac{\Box}{\Box}$ $\qquad$ _____

whole number

More Missing Terms

Write a proportion for each sentence and solve for the missing term.

<u>Sentence</u>	<u>Proportion</u>	<u>Missing Term</u>

1. 2 is to 5 as n is to 15

$$\frac{\boxed{}}{\boxed{}} = \frac{\boxed{}}{\boxed{}}$$

$n = \underline{\hspace{2cm}}$
whole number

2. n is to 35 as 1 is to 5

$$\frac{\boxed{}}{\boxed{}} = \frac{\boxed{}}{\boxed{}}$$

$\underline{\hspace{3cm}}$
whole number

3. n is to 4 as 6.4 is to 3.2

$$\frac{\boxed{}}{\boxed{}} = \frac{\boxed{}}{\boxed{}}$$

$\underline{\hspace{3cm}}$
whole number

4. 7 is to 4 as 10.5 is to n

$$\frac{\boxed{}}{\boxed{}} = \frac{\boxed{}}{\boxed{}}$$

$\underline{\hspace{3cm}}$
whole number

5. 5 is to 8 as n is to 32

$$\frac{\boxed{}}{\boxed{}} = \frac{\boxed{}}{\boxed{}}$$

$\underline{\hspace{3cm}}$
whole number

6. 7.45 is to 1 as n is to 5

$$\frac{\boxed{}}{\boxed{}} = \frac{\boxed{}}{\boxed{}}$$

$\underline{\hspace{3cm}}$
decimal

7. n is to 20 as 3 is to 8

$$\frac{\boxed{}}{\boxed{}} = \frac{\boxed{}}{\boxed{}}$$

$\underline{\hspace{3cm}}$
mixed number

8. n is to 5 as 12 is to 6

$$\frac{\boxed{}}{\boxed{}} = \frac{\boxed{}}{\boxed{}}$$

$\underline{\hspace{3cm}}$
whole number

Meaning of Proportion Review

Find the missing term in each proportion. Simplify first if necessary.

1. $\dfrac{5}{6} = \dfrac{15}{\boxed{}}$

2. $\dfrac{4}{8} = \dfrac{\boxed{}}{12}$

3. Write the proportion using fraction ratios.

9 is to 27 as 6 is to 18

$$\dfrac{\boxed{}}{\boxed{}} = \dfrac{\boxed{}}{\boxed{}}$$

4. Find the cross products.

$$\dfrac{7}{3} \quad = \quad \dfrac{21}{9}$$

$$\underline{} \times \underline{} = \underline{} \times \underline{}$$

$$\underline{} = \underline{}$$

5. Find the cross products and compare using = or ≠.

$$\dfrac{5}{8} \quad \bigcirc \quad \dfrac{40}{63}$$

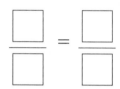

6. Find the missing term.

$$\dfrac{n}{30} = \dfrac{2}{5}$$

$$n \times 5 = 2 \times 30$$
$$n \times 5 = 60$$
$$n = 60 \div \underline{}$$
$$n = \underline{}$$

7. Solve for n.

$$\dfrac{4}{3} = \dfrac{20}{n}$$

8. Solve for n. Change the answer to a mixed number.

$$\dfrac{9}{n} = \dfrac{5}{6}$$

9. Use the cross-product method to solve the proportion.

$$\dfrac{n}{3} = \dfrac{4.15}{2.49}$$

Write a proportion and solve for n.

10. 7.25 is to 1 as n is to 6

11. n is to 4 as 15 is to 10

Proportions in Problem Solving

1. Read the problem carefully.
2. Represent the quantity you do not know by the letter n.
3. Write the units next to the numbers when writing the proportion.
4. Make sure the same units hold corresponding positions in the two ratios of the proportions.

Traveling at the rate of 110 miles in 2 hours, how far can you go in 5 hours?

The first ratio compares **miles** to **hours**: $\dfrac{110}{2}$ miles hours

The second ratio must also compare miles to hours: $\dfrac{n}{5}$ miles hours

The correct proportion is: $\dfrac{110}{2}$ miles hours $= \dfrac{n}{5}$ miles hours

---

Set up the proportion. **Do not solve.**

If 5 cans of soup cost \$6.50, how much will 9 cans of soup cost?

1. The first ratio compares ___cans___ to ___cost___ $\dfrac{5}{\$6.50}$ cans cost

2. The second ratio must also compare _____ to _____ $\dfrac{9}{\boxed{}}$ cans cost

3. The correct proportion is: $\dfrac{\boxed{}}{\boxed{}}$ cans cost $= \dfrac{\boxed{}}{\boxed{}}$

Setting Up Proportions

Make sure the same units hold corresponding positions in the two ratios of the proportion.

You can travel 28 miles on 2 gallons of gasoline. At the same rate, how far can you travel on 7 gallons of gasoline?

The first ratio compares miles to gallons.

$$\frac{28 \text{ miles}}{2 \text{ gallons}} = \frac{n \text{ miles}}{7 \text{ gallons}}$$

The second ratio must also compare miles to gallons.

Set up the proportions. Write in the numbers and the labels. **Do not solve.**

1. Kevin runs 3 miles in 24 minutes. At the same rate, how long does it take him to run 10 miles?

$$\frac{\boxed{} \text{ miles}}{\boxed{} \text{ minutes}} = \frac{\boxed{} \text{ miles}}{\boxed{} \text{ minutes}}$$

2. Jose drove 675 miles at an average speed of 45 miles per hour. How many hours did the trip take him? Remember, *per* means *each* or *one*.

$$\frac{\boxed{}\rule{1cm}{0.4pt}}{\boxed{}\rule{1cm}{0.4pt}} = \frac{\boxed{}\rule{1cm}{0.4pt}}{\boxed{}\rule{1cm}{0.4pt}}$$

3. Rocky got 2 hits for every 7 times at bat. He batted 56 times. How many hits did Rocky get?

$$\frac{\boxed{}\rule{1cm}{0.4pt}}{\boxed{}\rule{1cm}{0.4pt}} = \frac{\boxed{}\rule{1cm}{0.4pt}}{\boxed{}\rule{1cm}{0.4pt}}$$

4. 5 pounds of potatoes cost $3.95. How much will 13 pounds of potatoes cost?

$$\frac{\boxed{}\rule{1cm}{0.4pt}}{\boxed{}\rule{1cm}{0.4pt}} = \frac{\boxed{}\rule{1cm}{0.4pt}}{\boxed{}\rule{1cm}{0.4pt}}$$

Check Your Proportions

Write a proportion. Check each proportion to show that it is true.

If 2 eggs are needed to make 24 cookies, then 5 eggs will be needed to make 60 cookies.

<u>Proportion</u>

$$\frac{2 \text{ eggs}}{24 \text{ cookies}} = \frac{5 \text{ eggs}}{60 \text{ cookies}}$$

<u>Check</u>

$$\frac{2}{24} \diagdown\diagup \frac{5}{60}$$

$$2 \times 60 = 5 \times 24$$
$$120 = 120$$

Write proportions and check each answer.

1. 3 yards of material cost $5.94, so 2 yards of material will cost $3.96.

<u>Check</u>

2. Mr. Smith harvested 255 bushels of corn from 3 acres of land. At the same rate, he will harvest 1,700 bushels of corn from 20 acres.

<u>Check</u>

3. If 3 pounds of fertilizer cover 900 square feet, then 7 pounds of fertilizer will cover 2,100 square feet.

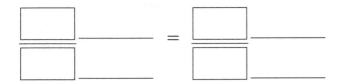

<u>Check</u>

4. Annette rode her bicycle 120 miles in 3 days. She bicycled 7 days at the same rate and traveled 280 miles.

<u>Check</u>

Using Proportions

A sports car owner gets 120 miles on 8 gallons of gasoline. How many miles can he travel on 28 gallons?

Proportion

$$\frac{120}{8} \begin{matrix} \text{miles} \\ \text{gallons} \end{matrix} = \frac{n}{28} \begin{matrix} \text{miles} \\ \text{gallons} \end{matrix}$$

Check

$$\frac{120}{8} \underset{\Large\times}{=} \frac{n}{28}$$

$$120 \times 28 = n \times 8$$
$$3{,}360 = n \times 8$$
$$n = 3{,}360 \div 8$$
$$n = 420 \text{ miles}$$

Use the proportions and solve each problem.

1. Boys outnumber girls by 3 to 2. If there are 56 girls, how many boys are there?

   Proportion   Solution

   $$\frac{3}{2} \begin{matrix} \text{boys} \\ \text{girls} \end{matrix} = \frac{n}{56} \begin{matrix} \text{boys} \\ \text{girls} \end{matrix}$$

2. Roast beef requires a cooking time of 25 minutes per pound. How many minutes would be required to cook a 6-pound roast?

   Proportion   Solution

   $$\frac{25}{1} \begin{matrix} \text{minutes} \\ \text{pound} \end{matrix} = \frac{n}{6} \begin{matrix} \text{minutes} \\ \text{pounds} \end{matrix}$$

3. Gilbert's car used 13 gallons of gasoline on a 273-mile trip. How many miles per gallon did his car get?

   Proportion   Solution

   $$\frac{13}{273} \begin{matrix} \text{gallons} \\ \text{miles} \end{matrix} = \frac{1}{n} \begin{matrix} \text{gallon} \\ \text{miles} \end{matrix}$$

4. Danna saved $245 in 5 weeks. At the same rate, how much will she save in 7 weeks?

   Proportion   Solution

   $$\frac{245}{5} \begin{matrix} \text{dollars} \\ \text{weeks} \end{matrix} = \frac{n}{7} \begin{matrix} \text{dollars} \\ \text{weeks} \end{matrix}$$

Unit Prices

Grocery stores often provide unit prices so that shoppers can compare different sizes of the same item. To find unit prices, you can use proportions.

> The **unit price** is the cost for one item or unit.

A 12-ounce can of orange juice costs $1.68.

Find the unit price.

$$\frac{12 \text{ ounces}}{\$1.68 \text{ cost}} = \frac{1 \text{ ounce}}{n \text{ cost}}$$

$$12 \times n = 1 \times 1.68$$

$$n = 1.68 \div 12$$

$$n = .14$$

The unit price is $.14 per ounce.

$7.20 for 6 pounds of bananas.

Find the unit price.

$$\frac{\$7.20 \text{ cost}}{6 \text{ pounds}} = \frac{n \text{ cost}}{1 \text{ pound}}$$

$$7.20 \times 1 = n \times 6$$

$$7.20 \div 6 = n$$

$$1.20 = n$$

The unit price is $1.20 per pound.

Find the unit prices.

Dishwashing Detergent

1. 32 ounces for $2.56

$$\frac{\boxed{} \text{ ounces}}{\boxed{} \text{ cost}} = \frac{\boxed{} \text{ ounce}}{\boxed{} \text{ cost}}$$

The unit price is $_____ per ounce.

Aspirin Tablets

3. $4.99 for 50 tablets

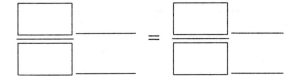

The unit price is $_____ per tablet.

Orange Juice

2. 6 ounces for $1.32

$$\frac{\boxed{}}{\boxed{}} = \frac{\boxed{}}{\boxed{}}$$

The unit price is $_____ per ounce.

Toothpaste

4. $2.94 for 7 ounces

$$\frac{\boxed{}}{\boxed{}} = \frac{\boxed{}}{\boxed{}}$$

The unit price is $_____ per ounce.

Find the Unit Costs

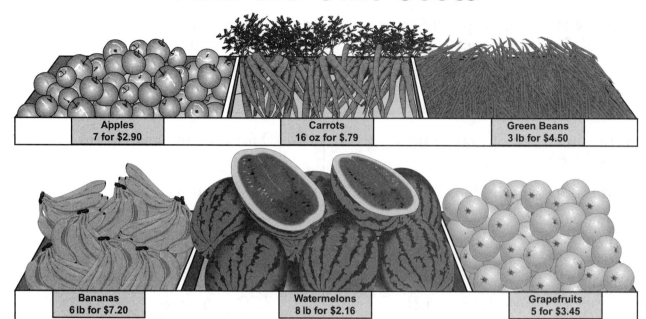

| Apples 7 for $2.90 | Carrots 16 oz for $.79 | Green Beans 3 lb for $4.50 |

| Bananas 6 lb for $7.20 | Watermelons 8 lb for $2.16 | Grapefruits 5 for $3.45 |

Use proportions to find the unit price of each item.

1. Bananas

$$\frac{\boxed{6} \text{ pounds}}{\boxed{7.20} \text{ dollars}} = \frac{\boxed{1} \text{ pound}}{\boxed{n} \text{ dollars}}$$

Unit price: $ _____ per pound

4. Green Beans

$$\frac{\boxed{}}{\boxed{}} = \frac{\boxed{}}{\boxed{}}$$

Unit price: $ _____ per pound

2. Watermelon

$$\frac{\boxed{}}{\boxed{}} = \frac{\boxed{}}{\boxed{n} \text{ dollars}}$$

Unit price: $ _____ per pound

5. Carrots

$$\frac{\boxed{}}{\boxed{}} = \frac{\boxed{}}{\boxed{}}$$

Unit price: $ _____ per ounce

3. Grapefruit

$$\frac{\boxed{}}{\boxed{}} = \frac{\boxed{}}{\boxed{}}$$

Unit price: $ _____ each

6. Apples

$$\frac{\boxed{}}{\boxed{}} = \frac{\boxed{}}{\boxed{}}$$

Unit price: $ _____ each

Comparison Shopping

Set up proportions and find the unit prices for two different sizes of a product. Compare the unit prices.

Shampoo

1. 9 ounces for $2.70

$$\frac{\boxed{9} \text{ ounces}}{\boxed{2.70} \text{ dollars}} = \frac{\boxed{1} \text{ ounce}}{\boxed{n} \text{ dollars}}$$

The unit price is $_____ per ounce.

15 ounces for $3.75

$$\frac{\boxed{}}{\boxed{}} = \frac{\boxed{1} \text{ ounce}}{\boxed{n} \text{ dollars}}$$

The unit price is $_____ per ounce.

Which size is cheaper per ounce? _____

Candy Bars

2. 6 for $3.42

$$\frac{\boxed{}}{\boxed{}} = \frac{\boxed{}}{\boxed{}}$$

The unit price is $_____ per bar.

3 for $1.56

$$\frac{\boxed{}}{\boxed{}} = \frac{\boxed{}}{\boxed{}}$$

The unit price is $_____ per bar.

Which package of candy bars is cheaper per bar? _____

Aluminum Foil

3. 200 feet for $6.00

$$\frac{\boxed{}}{\boxed{}} = \frac{\boxed{}}{\boxed{}}$$

The unit price is $_____ per foot.

25 feet for $1.00

$$\frac{\boxed{}}{\boxed{}} = \frac{\boxed{}}{\boxed{}}$$

The unit price is $_____ per foot.

Which size is cheaper per foot? _____

Potato Chips

4. 16 ounces for $2.56

$$\frac{\boxed{}}{\boxed{}} = \frac{\boxed{}}{\boxed{}}$$

The unit price is $_____ per ounce.

6 ounces for $1.32

$$\frac{\boxed{}}{\boxed{}} = \frac{\boxed{}}{\boxed{}}$$

The unit price is $_____ per ounce.

Which size is cheaper per ounce? _____

Proportion Applications Review

Set up the proportion. **Do not solve.**

1. Warren drove 330 miles at an average speed of 55 miles per hour. How many hours did the trip take him?

$$\frac{\boxed{}}{\boxed{}} = \frac{\boxed{}}{\boxed{}}$$

2. Amalia got 3 hits for every 8 times at bat. She batted 56 times. How many hits did Amalia get?

$$\frac{\boxed{}}{\boxed{}} = \frac{\boxed{}}{\boxed{}}$$

3. Victoria Farms regularily picks 235 bushels of apples from 2 acres of apple trees. At the same rate, how many bushels will be picked from 8 acres of trees?

$$\frac{\boxed{}}{\boxed{}} = \frac{\boxed{}}{\boxed{}}$$

4. Eight yards of cloth cost $21.36. How much will 12 yards cost?

$$\frac{\boxed{}}{\boxed{}} = \frac{\boxed{}}{\boxed{}}$$

Find the unit cost.

5. Twelve oranges for $1.56.

Unit Price: $_____ per orange

6. 16-ounce cup of coffee for $3.68

Unit Price: $_____ per ounce

7. 12-foot board for $12.36

Unit Price: $_____ per foot

8. 100 vitamins for $5.67

Unit Price: $_____ per vitamin

Changing Recipes

3 eggs are needed to make 15 waffles. How many eggs are needed to make 25 waffles?

Waffles
(makes approx 15 waffles)

3 eggs

4 tsp baking powder

$\frac{3}{4}$ tsp salt

$1\frac{3}{4}$ cups milk

1 tbsp melted shortening

A. $\dfrac{3}{15} \begin{smallmatrix}\text{eggs}\\\text{waffles}\end{smallmatrix} = \dfrac{n}{25} \begin{smallmatrix}\text{eggs}\\\text{waffles}\end{smallmatrix}$

$3 \times 25 = n \times 15$

$75 = n \times 15$

$75 \div 15 = n$

_____ $= n$

_____ eggs are needed to make 25 waffles.

---

1. 2 eggs are needed to make 24 cookies. How many eggs are needed to make 60 cookies?

_____ eggs are needed to make 60 cookies.

4. A soup recipe uses 3 teaspoons butter for 36 servings. How much butter is needed for 12 servings?

_____ teaspoon of butter is needed for 12 servings.

---

2. If a recipe uses 3 ounces of cream cheese to make 9 servings, then 4 ounces of cream cheese will make how many servings?

4 ounces of cream cheese will make _____ servings.

5. A pancake recipe calls for 6 tablespoons of milk for a serving of 4. How many servings will 9 tablespoons of milk make?

9 tablespoons of milk will make _____ servings.

---

3. A fruit punch recipe that serves 12 people calls for 4 oranges. How many oranges are needed to make punch for 18 people?

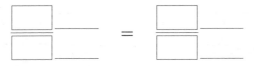

_____ oranges are needed to make punch for 18 people.

6. In a biscuit recipe 6 teaspoons of baking powder are needed to make 30 biscuits. How many teaspoons of baking powder are needed to make 40 biscuits?

_____ teaspoons of baking powder are needed to make 40 biscuits.

Figuring Costs

Two boxes of cereal cost $7.64. How much do five boxes of cereal cost?

2 for $7.64

A. $\dfrac{2}{7.64}\dfrac{\text{boxes}}{\text{dollars}} = \dfrac{5}{n}\dfrac{\text{boxes}}{\text{dollars}}$

$$2 \times n = 5 \times \$7.64$$
$$2 \times n = \$38.20$$
$$n = \$38.20 \div 2$$
$$n = \$_____$$

Five boxes of cereal cost $\$_____$.

To figure the costs, fill in the proportions and solve on another sheet of paper.

1. Material costs $4.80 per square yard. How much will 8 square yards cost?

$\dfrac{\boxed{}\ \text{dollars}}{\boxed{}\ \text{sq yd}} = \dfrac{\boxed{}\ \text{dollars}}{\boxed{}\ \text{sq yds}}$

8 square yards will cost $\$_____$.

2. Patricia bought 2 notebooks for $2.34. How many could she buy for $7.02?

$\dfrac{\boxed{}\ \_\_\_}{\boxed{}\ \_\_\_} = \dfrac{\boxed{}\ \_\_\_}{\boxed{}\ \_\_\_}$

Patricia could buy _____ notebooks for $7.02.

3. Craig bought 3 candy bars for $2.25. How much would 10 candy bars cost?

$\dfrac{\boxed{}\ \_\_\_}{\boxed{}\ \_\_\_} = \dfrac{\boxed{}\ \_\_\_}{\boxed{}\ \_\_\_}$

10 candy bars would cost $\$_____$.

4. 6 pounds of potatoes cost $1.50. How much will 13 pounds of potatoes cost?

$\dfrac{\boxed{}\ \_\_\_}{\boxed{}\ \_\_\_} = \dfrac{\boxed{}\ \_\_\_}{\boxed{}\ \_\_\_}$

13 pounds of potatoes will cost $\$_____$.

5. Sherlene bought 9 cans of soup that were marked 3 for $2.26. How much did she spend?

$\dfrac{\boxed{}\ \_\_\_}{\boxed{}\ \_\_\_} = \dfrac{\boxed{}\ \_\_\_}{\boxed{}\ \_\_\_}$

Sherlene spent $\$_____$ for 9 cans of soup.

6. If oranges cost $1.89 for 3, how much will 7 oranges cost?

$\dfrac{\boxed{}\ \_\_\_}{\boxed{}\ \_\_\_} = \dfrac{\boxed{}\ \_\_\_}{\boxed{}\ \_\_\_}$

7 oranges will cost $\$_____$.

Travel Plans

Kevin drives at an average speed of 55 miles per hour. How long will it take him to travel 385 miles?

SPEED LIMIT 55

A. $\dfrac{55 \text{ miles}}{1 \text{ hour}} = \dfrac{385 \text{ miles}}{n \text{ hour}}$

$55 \times n = 385 \times 1$

$55 \times n = 385$

$n = 385 \div 55$

$n = \underline{\hspace{1cm}}$

It will take Kevin _____ hours.

Use proportions to solve these travel problems.

1. A car averages 21 miles per gallon of gasoline. At this rate, how many gallons will be used on a 315-mile trip?

$$\frac{\boxed{}}{\boxed{}}\,\underline{} = \frac{\boxed{}}{\boxed{}}\,\underline{}$$

_____ gallons of gasoline will be used on a 315-mile trip.

2. A jet flies 1,365 miles in 3 hours. At the same rate of speed, how far can it fly in 5 hours?

$$\frac{\boxed{}}{\boxed{}}\,\underline{} = \frac{\boxed{}}{\boxed{}}\,\underline{}$$

The jet can fly _____ miles in 5 hours.

3. If a train can average 55 miles per hour, how many hours would it take the train to travel 220 miles?

$$\frac{\boxed{}}{\boxed{}}\,\underline{} = \frac{\boxed{}}{\boxed{}}\,\underline{}$$

It would take the train _____ hours to travel 220 miles.

4. A train travels at an average speed of 45 miles per hour. At the same rate, how far will it travel in 4.5 hours?

$$\frac{\boxed{}}{\boxed{}}\,\underline{} = \frac{\boxed{}}{\boxed{}}\,\underline{}$$

The train will travel _____ miles in 4.5 hours.

5. Carla paid $.40 to travel 25 miles on the toll road. At that rate, how much would it cost to travel 175 miles?

$$\frac{\boxed{}}{\boxed{}}\,\underline{} = \frac{\boxed{}}{\boxed{}}\,\underline{}$$

It would cost $_____ to travel 175 miles.

6. Ben traveled 104 miles in 2 hours. At this rate, how long will it take him to travel 260 miles?

$$\frac{\boxed{}}{\boxed{}}\,\underline{} = \frac{\boxed{}}{\boxed{}}\,\underline{}$$

It will take Ben _____ hours to travel 260 miles.

Scale Drawings

The scale (1 inch = 194 miles) for the Texas map is a ratio that compares the map distance to the actual distance.

1 inch on the map = **194 actual miles.**

The distance on the map between Dalhart and Houston is 3 inches. To find the actual distance in miles, set up a proportion.

$$\frac{1}{194} \begin{array}{l} \text{inch (map distance)} \\ \text{miles (actual distance)} \end{array} = \frac{3}{n} \begin{array}{l} \text{inches (map distance)} \\ \text{miles (actual distance)} \end{array}$$

$$1 \times n = 3 \times 194$$
$$n = 582$$

The actual distance is 582 miles.

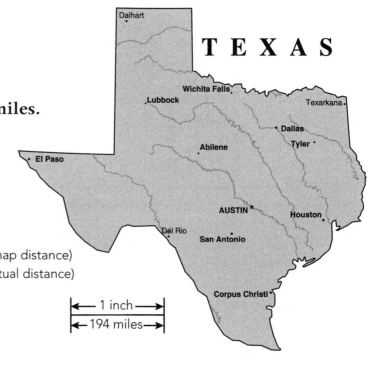

Set up proportions and solve. The map distances are given.

1. Find the actual distance between El Paso and San Antonio. The map distance is 2.5 inches.

$$\frac{1}{194} \begin{array}{l} \text{inch (map)} \\ \text{miles (actual)} \end{array} = \frac{2.5}{n} \begin{array}{l} \text{inches (map} \\ \text{miles (actual)} \end{array}$$

The actual distance between El Paso and San Antonio is _____ miles.

3. Find the actual distance between Wichita Falls and Corpus Christi. The map distance is 2 inches.

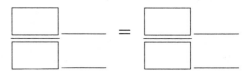

The actual distance between Wichita Falls and Corpus Christi is _____ miles.

---

2. Find the actual distance between Lubbock and Dallas. The map distance is 1.5 inches.

The actual distance between Lubbock and Dallas is _____ miles.

4. Find the actual distance between Texarkana and Tyler. The map distance is .5 of an inch.

The actual distance between Texarkana and Tyler is _____ miles.

Map Applications

Set up proportions and solve.

1. On a map, 1 inch equals 150 miles. How far is it between two cities that are 4 inches apart on the map?

$$\frac{\boxed{}}{\boxed{}} = \frac{\boxed{}}{\boxed{}}$$

The two cities are _____ miles apart.

2. On a map, 1 inch equals 45 miles. How many inches on the map would represent 315 miles?

$$\frac{\boxed{}}{\boxed{}} = \frac{\boxed{}}{\boxed{}}$$

_____ inches on the map represent 315 miles.

3. If a distance of 1 inch on a map equals 75 miles, what actual distance do 3 inches represent?

$$\frac{\boxed{}}{\boxed{}} = \frac{\boxed{}}{\boxed{}}$$

3 inches on the map represent _____ miles.

4. On a map, 2 inches equal 150 miles. What actual distance do 5 inches represent?

$$\frac{\boxed{}}{\boxed{}} = \frac{\boxed{}}{\boxed{}}$$

5 inches on the map represent _____ miles.

5. On a map of the United States, 2 inches equal 150 miles. How many inches will represent 375 miles?

$$\frac{\boxed{}}{\boxed{}} = \frac{\boxed{}}{\boxed{}}$$

375 miles are represented by _____ inches.

6. If 1.5 inches on a map equal 20 miles, how many miles will 6 inches represent?

$$\frac{\boxed{}}{\boxed{}} = \frac{\boxed{}}{\boxed{}}$$

6 inches on the map represent _____ miles.

7. On a map, each inch equals 150 miles. How far is it between two cities that are 3.5 inches apart?

$$\frac{\boxed{}}{\boxed{}} = \frac{\boxed{}}{\boxed{}}$$

It is _____ miles between two cities that are 3.5 inches apart.

8. A diagram shows $\frac{1}{2}$ inch (think .5) equals 50 miles. 7 inches on the scale equal how many miles?

$$\frac{\boxed{}}{\boxed{}} = \frac{\boxed{}}{\boxed{}}$$

7 inches on the scale equal _____ miles.

Make a Chart

Read the problem and decide what is being compared.

A recipe for salad dressing calls for mixing 5 tablespoons of oil to 2 tablespoons of vinegar. How many tablespoons of oil should you mix with 5 tablespoons of vinegar?

Compare oil to vinegar.

You can make a chart to organize your information.

oil	5	n
vinegar	2	5

Make a chart for the information. **Do not solve** for n.

1. Alice sleeps nine hours a day. How many hours does she sleep in a year? (Hint: 365 days in a year)

hours of sleep		
days		

3. On December 23, it snowed 1.5 inches an hour for 4 hours. How much did it snow in all?

2. For every $10 that Ellen earns, she saves $1. How much would Ellen save if she earned $155?

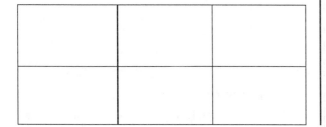

4. At Dan's school, 6 out of every 10 kids know how to swim. If there are 350 kids in his school, how many kids know how to swim?

Turn Charts into Proportions

Read the problem.

For every 2 pounds, roast beef requires a cooking time of 25 minutes. How many minutes are needed to cook a 6-pound roast?

pounds	2	6
minutes	25	n

The chart helps you set up your proportion. $\dfrac{2}{25} = \dfrac{6}{n}$

$$2 \times n = 6 \times 25$$
$$2 \times n = 150$$
$$n = 150 \div 2 = 75 \text{ minutes (1 hour and 15 minutes)}$$

Make a chart and write a proportion for each problem. Solve the proportion on another sheet of paper.

1. Larry gets a dollar bill for every 10 dimes that he takes to the bank. How many dollar bills will he get for 130 dimes?

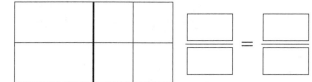

$n = $ _____

3. The snack mix recipe calls for 1.5 boxes of cereal for every bag of pretzels. How many boxes of cereal are needed if 3 bags of pretzels are being used?

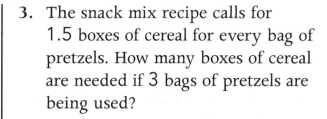

$n = $ _____

2. For every 6 tapes that you buy, you get 2 tapes free. If you bought nine tapes, how many free tapes would you get?

$n = $ _____

4. Janet has a cold. She can take 2 aspirin tablets every 4 hours. How many tablets can she take in 24 hours?

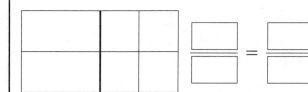

$n = $ _____

Proportions in Measurement

3 feet = 1 yard

How many feet
are in 6.5 yards?

<u>Set Up a Chart</u>

feet	3	n
yards	1	6.5

<u>Set Up a Proportion</u>

$\dfrac{3}{1}$ feet $= \dfrac{n}{6.5}$ feet
yard   yards

$3 \times 6.5 = n \times 1$

$19.5 = n$

There are 19.5 feet in 6.5 yards.

Use a chart to organize the information. Write a proportion and solve on
another sheet of paper.

1. 1 pound = 16 ounces.
   How many pounds are
   in 128 ounces?

pounds		
ounces		

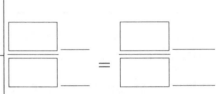

$n =$ _____

2. There are 4 pecks per
   bushel. How many
   pecks are in 52 bushels?

pecks		
bushels		

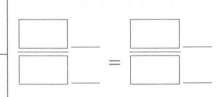

$n =$ _____

3. 1 gram = .04 ounce.
   How many ounces
   are in 564 grams?

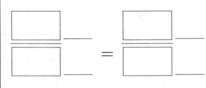

$n =$ _____

4. 100 centimeters =
   1 meter. How many
   centimeters are in
   655 meters?

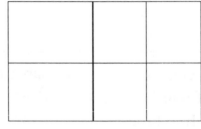

$n =$ _____

Proportions in Sports

Daniel runs 3 miles in 21 minutes. How long does it take him to run 8 miles at the same rate?

Set Up a Chart

miles	3	8
minutes	21	n

Write Up a Proportion

$$\frac{3}{21} = \frac{8}{n}$$

$3 \times n = 8 \times 21$

$3 \times n = 168$

$n = 168 \div 3$

$n = 56$ minutes

Use a chart to organize the information. Write a proportion and solve.

1. Dora rode her bicycle 120 miles in 3 days. She bicycled 7 days at the same rate. How far did she travel on her bicycle in 7 days?

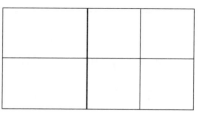

$n =$ _____

2. Edmund can walk 8.4 miles in 2 hours. At the same rate, how far can he walk in 3 hours?

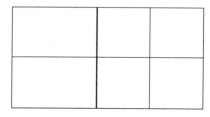

$n =$ _____

3. Riley hit 4 home runs in 6 games. At that rate, how many home runs could he hit in 9 games?

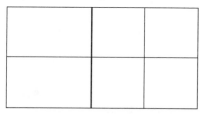

$n =$ _____

4. Wesley scored 92 points in 4 games. At the same rate, how many points could he score in 18 games?

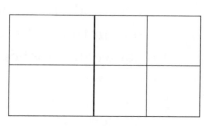

$n =$ _____

Proportion Problem-Solving Review

Solve each problem.

1. A recipe uses 6 teaspoons of vanilla to make 72 cookies. How many teaspoons of vanilla are needed to make 96 cookies?

   Answer: _____

2. Sol bought 5 pencils for $.75. How many pencils can he buy for $1.35?

   Answer: _____

3. It costs $.50 to travel 35 miles on the toll road. At that rate, how much would it cost to travel 122.5 miles?

   Answer: $_____

4. On a map of the United Kingdom, 1 inch equals 103 miles. How far is London from Edinburgh, a distance of 4 inches?

   Answer: _____

5. On a map, 2 inches equal 225 miles. How many inches will represent 1,350 miles?

   Answer: _____

6. Julio receives 5 dollars for every 20 quarters he saves. How many dollars will he receive for 140 quarters?

   Answer: _____

7. 1,000 millimeters = 1 meter. How many millimeters are in 2.5 meters?

   Answer: _____

8. Edwina scored 64 points in 4 games of basketball. At the same rate, how many points can she score in 15 games?

   Answer: _____

Write a simplified ratio.

1. 18 inches to 3 feet

2. 20 minutes to 1 hour

Answer: _____

Answer: _____

Solve the problems.

3. Joey replaced guitar strings for 3 hours. Out of 26 guitars, he replaced the strings on 8. What was the ratio between guitars fixed and hours worked?

Answer: _____

4. A survey showed that white cars outnumber blue cars by 7 to 2. If there were 189 white cars in the survey, how many blue cars were there?

Answer: _____

5. What is the unit price of a 16-ounce jar of spaghetti sauce that sells for $3.68?

Answer: $_____

6. Ella runs 4 miles in 32 minutes. How long does it take her to run 9 miles at the same rate?

Answer: _____

1. Write the ratio of 19 to 57 as a fraction and simplify.

   Answer: _____

2. Solve for m in $\frac{12}{7} = \frac{60}{m}$.

   Answer: _____

3. On Lou's map, $\frac{1}{2}$ inch = 60 miles. The distance between Denver and Pueblo is 1 inch. What is the actual distance?

   Answer: _____

4. Solve for x in $\frac{x}{4} = \frac{1}{3}$. Express the answer as a mixed number.

   Answer: _____

5. Simplify the ratio 45:54.

   Answer: _____

6. Carla surveyed 80 people about a new power plant. 45 people opposed the plant. What is the ratio of the people against the plant to the total number of people surveyed?

   Answer: _____

7. Write the ratio of 20 inches to 1 yard in simplest form.

   Answer: _____

8. Simplify the ratio 12:88.

   Answer: _____

9. Solve for a in $\frac{3.6}{12} = \frac{a}{4}$.

   Answer: _____

10. Curt saved $23 in one week. At the same rate, how many weeks will it take him to save $161?

    Answer: _____

11. Kevin runs 3 miles in 24 minutes. At the same rate, how long does it take him to run 1 mile?

Answer: _____

16. Write a proportion and solve for m in 8 is to 15 as m is to 9.

Answer: _____

12. Write the ratio of 15 minutes to 2 hours in simplest form.

Answer: _____

17. Simplify the ratio of 20 ounces to 1 pound.

Answer: _____

13. Solve for c in $\frac{8}{12} = \frac{c}{15}$.

Answer: _____

18. Jim repaired 17 cars in May and 23 in June. What is the ratio of the number of cars he repaired in May to the total number of cars he repaired?

Answer: _____

14. Two boxes of cereal cost $3.48. How much will 5 boxes of cereal cost?

Answer: $_____

19. On the highway, Marla drives at an average speed of 62 mph. At the same rate, how many hours will she need to drive 217 miles?

Answer: _____

15. Sarah got 3 questions wrong and 17 questions right on a quiz. What was the ratio of the questions wrong to the total number of questions?

Answer: _____

20. Helen makes $1,800 a month and pays $450 a month for rent. What is the ratio of her rent to the amount she makes?

Answer: _____

Evaluation Chart

On the following chart, circle the number of any problem you missed. The column after the problem number tells you the pages where those problems are taught. You should review the sections for any problem you missed.

Skill Area	Posttest Problem Number	Skill Section	Review Page
Meaning of Ratio	1, 5, 8	7–16	17
Ratio Applications	7, 12, 17	18–32	33
Ratio Problem Solving	15, 18, 20	34–41	42
Meaning of Proportion	2, 4, 9, 13, 16	43–55	56
Proportion Applications	All	57–63	64
Proportion Applications & Problem Solving	3, 6, 10, 11, 14, 19	65–73	74

acre an area of land

> My house was built on 2 acres of land.

average the sum of number divided by the total amount of number—another name for *mean*

> What is the average of 5, 7, 9, 12, and 2?
>
> $5 + 7 + 9 + 12 + 2 = 35$
>
> $35 \div 5 = 7$

cross product when the numerator of one fraction and the denominator of another fraction are multiplied and vice versa

$$\frac{6}{8} \overset{=}{\bowtie} \frac{3}{4}$$

$$6 \times 4 = 3 \times 8$$

$$24 = 24$$

denominator the bottom part of a fraction

$$\frac{5}{8} \leftarrow$$

ingredients the parts of a recipe

> I am going to the grocery store to buy the ingredients for chocolate cake.

number relation symbol symbols that explain the relationship between two numbers

> For example:
>
> | | |
> |---|---|
> | less than | $<$ |
> | greater than | $>$ |
> | equal to | $=$ |
> | not equal to | $\neq$ |
>
> 15 is greater than 9
>   **OR**
> $15 > 9$

order the specific arrangement of separate numbers or operations

> Put these letters in alphabetical order: C, A, D, B.
> A, B, C, D

per for each

> The grocery is charging 17¢ per banana.

proportion an expression made up of two equal ratios

$$\frac{1}{2} = \frac{5}{10}$$

ratio   a comparison of two numbers

> If John strikes out 2 of every
> 3 batters, the ratio of
> strikes to hits is 2:3.

simplify (reduce)   to make the number in a fraction smaller without changing the value of the fraction

$$\frac{2}{4} = \frac{1}{2} \qquad \frac{4}{6} = \frac{2}{3}$$

term   one of the numbers that makes up a ratio or fraction

$$\downarrow$$
$$2:3 \qquad \frac{1}{2} \leftarrow$$

unit price   the cost of one item or unit

> If 12 bananas cost $1.44, how
> much does each banana cost?

$$12\overline{)1.44}^{.12}$$

> The unit price of one banana
> is $.12.

unit rate   the rate for one unit of a given quantity

> The unit rate for electricity is 45¢
> per watt.